the Rainbow Bridge

by Steve Bodofsky

To our furry and feathered friends
who are waiting for us at the Bridge.
You will always be in our hearts.
We'll see you again one day.

By the edge of a woods,
at the foot of a hill,

Is a lush, green meadow
where time stands still.

Where the friends of man
and woman do run,

When their time on
earth is over and done.

For here, between
this world and the next,

Is a place where each
beloved creature finds rest.

On this golden land,
they wait and they play,
Till the Rainbow Bridge
they cross over one day.

No more do they suffer,
in pain or in sadness,
For here they are whole,
their lives filled with gladness.

Their limbs are restored,
their health renewed,

Their bodies have healed,
with strength imbued.

They romp through the grass,
without even a care,

Until one day they start,
and sniff at the air.

All ears prick forward,
eyes dart front and back,

Then all of a sudden
one breaks from the pack.

For just at that instant,
their eyes have met;

Together again, both
person and pet.

So they run to each other,
these friends from long past,
The time of their parting
is over at last.

The sadness they felt
while they were apart,

Has turned to joy
once more in each heart.

They embrace with a love
that will last forever...

And then, side-by-side,
they cross over…
together.

The End

The Rainbow Bridge

inspired by a Norse legend

By the edge of a woods, at the foot of a hill,
Is a lush, green meadow where time stands still.
Where the friends of man and woman do run,
When their time on earth is over and done

For here, between this world and the next,
Is a place where each beloved creature finds rest.
On this golden land, they wait and they play,
Till the Rainbow Bridge they cross over one day.

No more do they suffer, in pain or in sadness,
For here they are whole, their lives filled with gladness.
Their limbs are restored, their health renewed,
Their bodies have healed, with strength imbued.

They romp through the grass, without even a care,
Until one day they start, and sniff at the air.
All ears prick forward, eyes dart front and back,
Then all of a sudden, one breaks from the pack.

For just at that instant, their eyes have met;
Together again, both person and pet.
So they run to each other, these friends from long past,
The time of their parting is over at last.

The sadness they felt while they were apart,
Has turned into joy once more in each heart.
They embrace with a love that will last forever,
And then, side-by-side, they cross over… together.

Final thoughts by the Author,

For many people, the passing of a pet can be the most devastating loss they've ever experienced.

Think that's an overstatement?

Consider this: When you lose a family member – a human one – you can usually expect support from people in every area of your life. Your employer expects you to take time off for bereavement. Your friends and family offer condolences; many will attend the funeral or other memorials. And your church is likely to promise eternal reward.

But when you lose a pet, all that changes. Try to take a day off from work because your dog passed; you're likely to be told not to bother coming back. Your friends may tell you to "just buy another one." Your church leader may even suggest that pets have no souls, so you won't be seeing them again.

For many people, a pet is a family member. In the case of children, that pet may have been part of the family since before they were born. They never knew a time when Rover or Mittens wasn't part of their family, so their passing marks the end of a chapter in their own lives. To them, they lost a shorter, fuzzier brother or sister.

But – and this may be the worst part of all – you can never be sure how someone else will respond to your grief. So most people learn not to share their sorrow: They hold it in… keep it to themselves.

For those people suffering the loss of a furry friend, young and old alike, we offer the Rainbow Bridge: a promise for reunion and a future shared. A place of health and happiness forever.

We hope it brings you comfort.

The Rainbow Bridge
Written by Steve Bodofsky
Illustrated by Martina S. Kaiser
Designed by Bruce Kaiser

Steve Bodofsky is a writer and producer. He and his wife, Diane, have owned and operated the Last Chance Ferret Rescue for nearly 30 years, where they've cared for and rehomed hundreds of unwanted ferrets. Visit them on line at www.NewRainbow-Bridge.com.

Martina Kaiser, or Tina as her friends know her, has a degree in advertising design and artwork, and has worked for a number of advertising agencies. Tina enjoys drawing and painting animals and landscapes. Recently, she has been specializing in capturing the love and care of mother animals for their babies in the wild. Her goal is for her paintings to help raise awareness of the desperate plight of animals in the wild. Her other passion has been singing and entertaining, first as a child on local TV, later in musical comedies and bands.

Bruce Kaiser has an education in graphic design and commercial illustration. He's worked for area design firms and has freelanced for many years. He also paints, specializing in classic cars and Americana. www.kaisercarart.com.

Martina and Bruce have a son, Warren. They live in upstate New York with their two crazy Westies, Mac and Tessa.

Website	www.newrainbowbridge.com
Facebook	@rainbowbridgebook
Google+	https://plus.google.com/collection/UChSbF
Twitter	@NewRainbowBrid1
Pinterest	www.pinterest.com/59ce757cde0c328d41b02cba4affe0

Printed in Great Britain
by Amazon